MW01234116

5 INGREDIL

COOKBOOK

"Easy Low-Carb Recipes with Few

Ingredients"

ALLIE NAGEL

Copyright © 2023 by Allie Nagel

All rights reserved. No part of this book may be reproduced, stored, or transmitted by any means whether auditory, graphic, mechanical, or electronic without written permission of the author, except in the case of brief excerpts used in critical articles and reviews.

Any people depicted in stock imagery are models, and such images are being used for illustrative purposes only.

DISCLAIMER

This cookbook is intended to provide general information and recipes.

The recipes provided in this cookbook are not intended to replace or be a substitute for medical advice from a physician.

The reader should consult a healthcare professional for any specific medical advice, diagnosis or treatment.

Any specific dietary advice provided in this cookbook is not intended to replace or be a substitute for medical advice from a physician.

The author is not responsible or liable for any adverse effects experienced by readers of this cookbook as a result of following the recipes or dietary advice provided.

The author makes no representations or warranties of any kind (express or implied) as to the accuracy, completeness, reliability or suitability of the recipes provided in this cookbook.

The author disclaims any and all liability for any damages arising out of the use or misuse of the recipes provided in this cookbook. The reader must also take care to ensure that the recipes provided in this cookbook are prepared and cooked safely.

The recipes provided in this cookbook are for informational purposes only and should not be used as a substitute for professional medical advice, diagnosis or treatment.

TABLE OF CONTENTS

INTRODUCTION

Low-carb have gained popularity as a dietary approach aimed at weight management and improved health.

These diets typically limit the intake of carbohydrates, emphasizing a higher consumption of protein and healthy fats.

One of the primary goals of low-carb diets is to induce a state of ketosis, where the body relies on fat as its primary fuel source instead of carbohydrates.

This metabolic shift is believed to promote weight loss by burning stored fat for energy. Additionally, low-carb diets may help regulate blood sugar levels, making them a potential option for you with type 2 diabetes or insulin resistance.

Common foods in low-carb diets include lean proteins like meat, poultry, fish, eggs, and non-starchy vegetables.

Foods high in refined sugars and grains, such as bread, pasta, and sweets, are restricted to minimize carbohydrate intake. Some variations of low-carb diets, like the ketogenic diet, have more specific guidelines, often requiring a very low daily carbohydrate intake, typically below 50 grams.

Research suggests that low-carb diets may lead to significant initial weight loss, improvements in blood lipid profiles, and enhanced insulin sensitivity.

However, long-term adherence to these diets can be challenging and concerns exist about potential nutrient deficiencies and the exclusion of certain food groups that provide essential nutrients and dietary fiber.

individual responses to low-carb diets vary, and consulting with healthcare professionals or nutritionists is advisable before embarking on such dietary changes.

Finally, it's crucial to prioritize nutrient-dense, whole foods and consider the long-term sustainability of any diet plan.

As with any dietary approach, balance, variety, and moderation are key factors in promoting overall health and well-being.

CHAPTER 1

BENEFITS OF A 5 INGREDIENT LOW CARB DIET

1. **Weight Loss:** Low-carb diets are often effective for weight loss, as they help reduce overall calorie intake and promote the burning of stored fat.

2. **Improved Blood Sugar Control:** Lowering carbohydrate intake can lead to better blood sugar control, making it beneficial for individuals with insulin resistance or diabetes.

3. **Increased Satiety:** Foods high in healthy fats and proteins can help you feel fuller for longer periods, reducing the likelihood of overeating.

4. **Enhanced Mental Clarity:** Some people report improved mental focus and clarity when following a low-carb diet, which may be attributed to stable blood sugar levels.

5. **Reduced Cravings:** Cutting back on refined carbohydrates can help reduce cravings for sugary and processed foods, making it easier to stick to a healthy eating plan.

6. **Improved Triglyceride Levels:** Low-carb diets have been associated with lower levels of triglycerides, a type of fat in the blood that, when elevated, can contribute to cardiovascular issues.

7. **Increased HDL Cholesterol:** A low-carb diet may lead to an increase in high-density lipoprotein (HDL) cholesterol, often referred to as "good" cholesterol.

8. **Better Blood Pressure Management:** Some studies suggest that a low-carb diet may contribute to lower blood pressure levels, reducing the risk of cardiovascular diseases.

9. **Stable Energy Levels:** By avoiding the peaks and crashes in blood sugar associated with high-carb meals, individuals on a low-carb diet may experience more stable energy levels throughout the day.

10. **Enhanced Fat Burning:** The body shifts to burning fat for energy in the absence of high carbohydrate intake, which can contribute to weight loss and improved body composition.

11. **Reduced Inflammation:** Some research suggests that low-carb diets may help reduce markers of

inflammation in the body, which is associated with various chronic diseases.

12. **Improved Insulin Sensitivity:** Lowering carbohydrate intake can enhance insulin sensitivity, making it easier for the body to regulate blood sugar levels.

13. **Better Control of Hunger Hormones:** A low-carb diet can positively impact hormones like ghrelin and leptin, helping to regulate hunger and satiety.

14. **Management of Metabolic Syndrome:** A low-carb diet may be beneficial for individuals with metabolic syndrome, a cluster of conditions that increase the risk of heart disease, stroke, and type 2 diabetes.

15. **Support for Epilepsy Treatment:** Low-carb diets, such as the ketogenic diet, have been used as a therapeutic approach to manage epilepsy, particularly in children.

TIPS AND TRICKS ON HOW TO FOLLOW A 5 INGREDIENT LOW CARB DIET

1. **Plan Meals Ahead:** Plan your meals in advance to ensure you have the necessary ingredients and can avoid last-minute, less healthy choices.

2. **Stock Up on Staples:** Keep your kitchen stocked with low-carb staples such as eggs, avocados, olive oil, lean meats, and non-starchy vegetables.

3. **Read Labels:** When purchasing packaged foods, carefully read labels to identify hidden sugars and high-carb ingredients. Choose products with minimal, recognizable ingredients.

4. **Embrace Simple Recipes:** Focus on uncomplicated recipes with just a few ingredients. This minimizes the chance of straying from your low-carb goals and makes meal preparation easier.

5. **Batch Cooking:** Prepare larger quantities of low-carb meals and portion them for the week. This can save time and make it convenient to stick to your dietary plan.

6. **Learn Portion Control:** While low-carb foods can be healthy, portion control is still crucial for managing caloric intake. Be mindful of serving sizes.

7. **Include Healthy Fats:** Incorporate sources of healthy fats such as avocados, olive oil, nuts, and seeds to add flavor and increase satiety.

8. **Snack Smart:** Choose low-carb snacks like cheese, nuts, or vegetables with dip to keep hunger at bay between meals.

9. **Explore Low-Carb Alternatives:** Find and experiment with low-carb alternatives for your favorite high-carb foods, such as cauliflower rice instead of regular rice or zucchini noodles instead of pasta.

10. **Limit Processed Foods:** Minimize your intake of processed and packaged foods, as they may contain hidden sugars and additives that can undermine your low-carb efforts.

11. **Social Support:** Inform friends and family about your dietary choices to receive support. Sharing your goals can also help avoid tempting situations.

12. **Educate Yourself:** Learn about the nutritional content of different foods to make informed choices. Understanding which foods are low in carbs can make grocery shopping and meal planning easier.

14 ESSENTIAL KITCHEN ITEMS NEEDED TO MAKE A 5 INGREDIENT LOW CARB DIET

1. **Chef's Knife:** A versatile and sharp chef's knife is crucial for chopping vegetables, cutting meats, and preparing various ingredients.

2. **Cutting Board:** Use a durable and spacious cutting board to chop, slice, and dice vegetables, meats, and other low-carb ingredients.

3. **Vegetable Spiralizer:** This tool is handy for turning vegetables like zucchini or cucumbers into low-carb noodles or spirals, offering a carb-friendly alternative to traditional pasta.

4. **Quality Frying Pan/Skillet:** A non-stick or well-seasoned frying pan is essential for cooking proteins and sautéing vegetables with minimal oil.

5. **Baking Sheet:** Use a baking sheet for roasting low-carb vegetables or baking protein sources for an easy and hands-off cooking method.

6. **Blender/Food Processor:** A blender or food processor is useful for creating smoothies, sauces, or pureeing vegetables for soups while keeping your ingredient list minimal.

7. **Measuring Cups and Spoons:** Accurate measurement is crucial in a low-carb diet. Have a set of measuring cups and spoons for precise portions.

8. **Digital Food Scale:** For even more accurate measurements, a digital food scale can help you control your carb intake and maintain proper portion sizes.

9. **Non-Stick Cooking Spray or Olive Oil Sprayer:** Keep your cooking low in added fats by using a non-stick spray or olive oil sprayer for light coating when necessary.

10. **Sauté Pan:** A sauté pan with high sides is excellent for cooking one-pan meals and stir-frying vegetables and proteins together.

11. **Grill Pan or Outdoor Grill:** Grilling adds a smoky flavor to meats and vegetables without the need for excess fats. A grill pan is suitable for indoor cooking.

12. **Mixing Bowls:** Have a set of mixing bowls in various sizes for combining ingredients, tossing salads, or marinating proteins.

13. **Cheese Grater:** Grate your own cheese to control portions and avoid added starches or fillers often found in pre-shredded cheese.

14. **Silicone Baking Mats:** These mats are a non-stick and reusable alternative to parchment paper, making cleanup easy when baking low-carb treats.

CHAPTER 3

14-DAY MEAL PLAN

DAY 1

Breakfast: Avocado and Green Bean Eggs

Lunch: Chicken Cobb Salad

Dinner: Greek Yogurt Chicken Salad with Stuffed Pepper

DAY 2

Breakfast: Scrambled Eggs with Carrot Sauce

Lunch: Garlic Herb Shrimp and Salmon

Dinner: Chicken Caesar Salad

DAY 3

Breakfast: Baked Green Eggs

Lunch: Coconut Curry Cooked Wild Rice

Dinner: Turkey Meatballs with Zucchini Noodles

DAY 4

Breakfast: Healthy Bell Pepper, Tomato, and Ham Omelet

Lunch: Avocado Chicken Salad

Dinner: Chicken Meatballs with Coconut Herb Sauce

DAY 5

Breakfast: Dark Chocolate Chia Pudding

Lunch: Pesto Chicken and Low Carb Veggies

Dinner: Zoodle Stir Fry

DAY 6

Breakfast: Tofu Scramble

Lunch: Cucumber, Tomato, and Avocado Salad

Dinner: Kung Pao Chicken

DAY 7

Breakfast: Chia Pudding

Lunch: Salmon and Broccoli Veggie

Dinner: Keto Pasta with Lemon Kale Chicken

DAY 8

Breakfast: Kimchi Scramble Eggs

Lunch: Cajun Shrimp and Sausage

Dinner: Mini Eggplant Pizza

DAY 9

Breakfast: Smoked Salmon with Asparagus Salad

Lunch: Chicken and Avocado Salad with Lime and Cilantro

Dinner: Broccoli, Asparagus, and Celery Salad

DAY 10

Breakfast: Keto Breakfast Burrito

Lunch: Cauliflower Broccoli Ham Salad

Dinner: Spicy Lemon Ginger Chicken Soup

DAY 11

Breakfast: Avocado and Green Bean Eggs

Lunch: Chicken Cobb Salad

Dinner: Greek Yogurt Chicken Salad with Stuffed Pepper

DAY 12

Breakfast: Scrambled Eggs with Carrot Sauce

Lunch: Garlic Herb Shrimp and Salmon

Dinner: Chicken Caesar Salad

DAY 13

Breakfast: Baked Green Eggs

Lunch: Coconut Curry Cooked Wild Rice

Dinner: Turkey Meatballs with Zucchini Noodles

DAY 14

Breakfast: Healthy Bell Pepper, Tomato, and Ham Omelet

Lunch: Avocado Chicken Salad

Dinner: Chicken Meatballs with Coconut Herb Sauce

30 NUTRITIOUS RECIPES FOR A 5 INGREDIENT LOW CARB DIET

BREAKFAST

Avocado and Green Bean Eggs

Preparation Time: 15 minutes

Serves: 2

Calories: 300

Ingredients:

Avocado

Green beans

Eggs

Olive oil

Salt and pepper to taste

Method of Preparation:

1. Cut the avocado in half, remove the pit, and slice the flesh.

2. Boil or steam the green beans until they are tender but still crisp. Drain and set aside.

3. In a pan, heat olive oil over medium heat. Crack the eggs into the pan and cook to your desired doneness (scrambled or fried).

4. Place the cooked eggs on a plate, arrange sliced avocados and blanched green beans on the side.

5. Sprinkle salt and pepper to taste.

Scrambled Eggs with Carrot Sauce

Preparation Time: 20 minutes

Serves: 2

Calories: 250

Ingredients:

Eggs

Carrots

Butter

Fresh parsley (optional, for garnish)

Salt and pepper to taste

Method of Preparation:

1. Peel and grate the carrots.
2. In a pan, melt butter over medium heat. Add grated carrots and sauté until they are soft and slightly caramelized.
3. Push the carrots to one side of the pan and crack the eggs into the other side. Scramble the eggs until fully cooked.
4. Mix the scrambled eggs with the carrot sauce.
5. Garnish with fresh parsley if desired. Add salt and pepper to taste.

Baked Green Eggs

Preparation Time: 25 minutes

Serves: 2

Calories: 280

Ingredients:

Eggs

Spinach

Feta cheese

Olive oil

Salt and pepper to taste

Method of Preparation:

1. Preheat the oven to 375°F (190°C).
2. Steam or sauté the spinach until wilted. Drain any excess liquid.
3. Grease a baking dish with olive oil.
4. Spread the wilted spinach evenly in the baking dish. Crack eggs on top of the spinach.
5. Crumble feta cheese over the eggs. Season with salt and pepper.
6. Bake in the preheated oven for about 15-20 minutes or until the egg whites are set but the yolks are still runny.

Healthy Bell Pepper, Tomato, and Ham Omelet

Preparation Time: 15 minutes

Serves:2

Calories: 250 **Sugar:** 3g **Sodium:** 500mg

Ingredients:

Eggs (4)

Bell peppers (mixed colors, 1 cup, chopped)

Cherry tomatoes (1/2 cup, halved)

Ham (1/2 cup, diced)

Olive oil (1 tablespoon)

Method of Preparation:

1. In a bowl, beat the eggs and season with salt and pepper.
2. Heat olive oil in a non-stick pan over medium heat.
3. Add the chopped bell peppers and cook until slightly softened.
4. Add ham to the pan and cook for an additional 2-3 minutes.
5. Pour the beaten eggs over the ingredients in the pan.
6. Scatter halved cherry tomatoes on top.

7. Allow the eggs to set on the bottom, then gently lift the edges to let uncooked eggs flow underneath.

8. Once the omelet is mostly set, fold it in half and cook until the eggs are fully cooked.

9. Serve hot.

Dark Chocolate Chia Pudding

Preparation Time: 10 minutes (+ refrigeration time)

Serves: 2

Calories: 180 **Sugar:** 2g **Sodium:** 50mg

Ingredients:

Chia seeds (1/4 cup)

Unsweetened almond milk (1 cup)

Dark chocolate (70% cocoa, 2 oz, melted)

Vanilla extract (1 teaspoon)

Low-carb sweetener (to taste)

Method of Preparation:

1. In a bowl, mix chia seeds and almond milk. Let it sit for 10 minutes, stirring occasionally.

2. Stir in melted dark chocolate and vanilla extract.

3. Sweeten to taste with your preferred low-carb sweetener.

4. Cover the bowl and refrigerate for at least 2 hours or overnight.

5. Before serving, stir well and adjust sweetness if needed.

Tofu Scramble

Preparation Time: 15 minutes

Serves: 2

Calories: 220 **Sugar:** 2g **Sodium:** 300mg

Ingredients:

Firm tofu (1 block, crumbled)

Spinach (1 cup, chopped)

Cherry tomatoes (1/2 cup, halved)

Turmeric powder (1/2 teaspoon)

Olive oil (1 tablespoon)

Method of Preparation:

1. Heat olive oil in a pan over medium heat.
2. Add crumbled tofu and turmeric powder. Cook for 5-7 minutes, stirring occasionally.
3. Add chopped spinach and halved cherry tomatoes. Cook for an additional 3-5 minutes until the vegetables are tender.
4. Season with salt and pepper to taste.
5. Serve hot.

Chia Pudding

Preparation Time: 5 minutes

Serves: 2

Calories: 120 **Sugar:** 1g **Sodium:** 80mg

Ingredients:

1/4 cup chia seeds

1 cup unsweetened almond milk

1 tablespoon sugar-free sweetener (e.g., stevia or erythritol)

1/2 teaspoon vanilla extract

Berries for topping (optional)

Method of Preparation:

1. In a bowl, mix chia seeds, almond milk, sweetener, and vanilla extract.
2. Stir well to ensure chia seeds are evenly distributed.
3. Let it sit for 10 minutes, stirring occasionally to prevent clumping.
4. Refrigerate for at least 2 hours or overnight until it thickens.
5. Top with berries before serving.

Kimchi Scramble Eggs

Preparation Time: 10 minutes

Serves: 2

Calories: 220 **Sugar:** 1g **Sodium:** 350mg

Ingredients:

4 eggs

1/2 cup kimchi, chopped

2 tablespoons butter or olive oil

Salt and pepper to taste

Chopped green onions for garnish (optional)

Method of Preparation:

1. Whisk the eggs in a bowl and season with salt and pepper.
2. Heat butter or olive oil in a pan over medium heat.
3. Add chopped kimchi to the pan and sauté for 1-2 minutes.
4. Pour whisked eggs into the pan and scramble until cooked.
5. Garnish with chopped green onions if desired.

Smoked Salmon with Asparagus Salad

Preparation Time: 15 minutes

Serves: 2

Calories: 250 **Sugar:** 0.5g **Sodium:** 500mg

Ingredients:

150g smoked salmon

1 bunch asparagus, trimmed

1 tablespoon olive oil

1 tablespoon lemon juice

Salt and pepper to taste

Method of Preparation:

1. Steam or blanch asparagus until tender-crisp, then let it cool.
2. Arrange smoked salmon on a plate.
3. Place asparagus on top of the smoked salmon.
4. In a small bowl, mix olive oil, lemon juice, salt, and pepper for dressing.
5. Drizzle dressing over the asparagus and salmon.

Keto Breakfast Burrito

Preparation Time: 10 minutes

Serves: 2

Calories: 300 **Sugar:** 1g **Sodium:** 600mg

Ingredients:

2 large eggs

2 low-carb tortillas

1/2 cup cooked and crumbled sausage or bacon

1/4 cup shredded cheese

2 tablespoons salsa (sugar-free)

Method of Preparation:

1. Scramble eggs in a pan until fully cooked.
2. Warm tortillas in a dry skillet or microwave.
3. Divide scrambled eggs, sausage or bacon, cheese, and salsa between the tortillas.
4. Fold the sides of each tortilla and roll to create a burrito.
5. Optional: Grill the burrito for a crispy texture.

LUNCH

Chicken Cobb Salad

Preparation Time: 20 minutes

Serves: 2

Calories: 400 **Sugar:** 3g **Sodium:** 600mg

Ingredients:

Chicken breast (grilled and sliced)

Mixed salad greens

Cherry tomatoes (halved)

Avocado (sliced)

Blue cheese dressing

Method of Preparation:

1. Grill the chicken breast until fully cooked, then slice it into strips.
2. In a large bowl, combine mixed salad greens, cherry tomatoes, and sliced avocado.
3. Add the grilled chicken strips to the salad.
4. Drizzle the blue cheese dressing over the salad and toss gently to combine.
5. Serve immediately.

Garlic Herb Shrimp and Salmon

Preparation Time: 20 minutes

Serves: 2

Calories: 350 **Sugar:** 0g **Sodium:** 300mg

Ingredients:

Shrimp (peeled and deveined)

Salmon fillets

Garlic (minced)

Fresh herbs (such as parsley or dill, chopped)

Olive oil

Method of Preparation:

1. Preheat the oven to 400°F (200°C).
2. Place shrimp and salmon fillets on a baking sheet.
3. In a bowl, mix minced garlic, fresh herbs, and olive oil. Drizzle the mixture over the shrimp and salmon.
4. Bake in the preheated oven for 12-15 minutes or until the seafood is cooked through.
5. Serve hot.

Coconut Curry Cooked Wild Rice

Preparation Time: 25 minutes

Serves: 2

Calories: 300 **Sugar:** 3g **Sodium:** 150mg

Ingredients:

Wild rice (cooked)

Coconut milk

Curry powder

Spinach (fresh or frozen)

Red bell pepper (sliced)

Method of Preparation:

1. Cook the wild rice according to package instructions.
2. In a saucepan, combine coconut milk and curry powder. Heat over medium heat.
3. Add cooked wild rice, spinach, and sliced red bell pepper to the coconut curry mixture.
4. Stir until well combined and heated through.
5. Serve warm.

Avocado Chicken Salad

Preparation Time: 25 Minutes

Serves: 4

Calories: 350 **Sugar:** 2g **Sodium:** 150mg

Ingredients:

Chicken breast (boneless, skinless) - 1 pound

Avocado - 2 ripe ones

Cherry tomatoes - 1 cup, halved

Olive oil - 2 tablespoons

Lemon juice - 1 tablespoon

Method of Preparation:

1. Grill or pan-cook the chicken breast until fully cooked.
2. Dice the cooked chicken into bite-sized pieces.
3. Cut the avocados into cubes.
4. In a large bowl, combine the diced chicken, avocado cubes, and halved cherry tomatoes.
5. In a small bowl, whisk together olive oil and lemon juice to create the dressing.
6. Drizzle the dressing over the chicken and avocado mixture. Gently toss until well coated.
7. Season with salt and pepper to taste.
8. Serve immediately.

Pesto Chicken and Low Carb Veggies

Preparation Time: 30 Minutes

Serves: 4

Calories: 400 **Sugar:** 3g **Sodium:** 250mg

Ingredients:

Chicken thighs (boneless, skinless) - 1 pound

Pesto sauce - 1/2 cup

Broccoli florets - 2 cups

Cherry tomatoes - 1 cup, halved

Olive oil - 2 tablespoons

Method of Preparation:

1. Preheat the oven to 400°F (200°C).
2. Place chicken thighs in a baking dish.
3. Spread pesto sauce over each chicken thigh.
4. In a bowl, toss broccoli florets and cherry tomatoes with olive oil.

5. Arrange the coated veggies around the chicken in the baking dish.

6. Bake in the preheated oven for 25-30 minutes or until the chicken is cooked through.

7. Serve hot.

Cucumber, Tomato and Avocado Salad

Preparation Time: 15 Minutes

Serves: 4

Calories: 250 **Sugar:** 4g **Sodium:** 200mg

Ingredients:

Cucumbers - 2, thinly sliced

Cherry tomatoes - 1 cup, halved

Avocado - 1, diced

Feta cheese - 1/2 cup, crumbled

Olive oil - 2 tablespoons

Method of Preparation:

1. In a large bowl, combine sliced cucumbers, halved cherry tomatoes, diced avocado, and crumbled feta cheese.
2. Drizzle olive oil over the salad.
3. Gently toss until all ingredients are well mixed.
4. Season with salt and pepper to taste.
5. Refrigerate for at least 30 minutes before serving to allow flavors to meld.
6. Serve chilled.

Salmon and Broccoli Veggie

Preparation Time: 25 minutes

Serves: 2

Calories: 350

Ingredients:

Salmon fillets

Broccoli florets

Olive oil

Garlic (minced)

Lemon juice

Method of Preparation:

1. Preheat the oven to 400°F (200°C).
2. Place salmon fillets on a baking sheet lined with parchment paper.
3. In a bowl, toss broccoli florets with olive oil and minced garlic.
4. Arrange broccoli around the salmon on the baking sheet.
5. Drizzle lemon juice over the salmon and broccoli.
6. Bake in the preheated oven for 15-20 minutes or until salmon is cooked through and flakes easily.
7. Serve hot.

Cajun Shrimp and Sausage

Preparation Time: 20 minutes

Serves: 4

Calories: 300

Ingredients:

Shrimp (peeled and deveined)

Smoked sausage (sliced)

Cajun seasoning

Olive oil

Bell peppers (sliced)

Method of Preparation:

1. Heat olive oil in a skillet over medium heat.
2. Add sliced sausage and cook until browned.
3. Toss in shrimp and sliced bell peppers.
4. Sprinkle Cajun seasoning over the mixture.
5. Cook until shrimp are opaque and cooked through.
6. Serve hot.

Chicken and Avocado Salad with Lime and Cilantro

Preparation Time: 15 minutes

Serves: 2

Calories: 300 **Sodium:** 250mg

Ingredients:

Chicken breasts (grilled and sliced)

Avocado (sliced)

Lime juice

Cilantro (chopped)

Salt and pepper to taste

Method of Preparation:

1. In a bowl, combine sliced grilled chicken and avocado.
2. Drizzle lime juice over the mixture.
3. Sprinkle chopped cilantro, salt, and pepper.
4. Toss gently until well combined.
5. Serve chilled.

Cauliflower Broccoli Ham Salad

Preparation Time: 15 minutes

Serves: 4

Calories: 200

Ingredients:

Cauliflower florets (steamed)

Broccoli florets (steamed)

Ham (diced)

Mayonnaise

Mustard

Method of Preparation:

1. In a large bowl, combine steamed cauliflower and broccoli.
2. Add diced ham to the bowl.
3. In a small bowl, mix mayonnaise and mustard to make the dressing.
4. Pour the dressing over the vegetables and ham.
5. Toss gently until everything is well coated.
6. Serve chilled.

DINNER

Greek Yogurt Chicken Salad with Stuffed Pepper

Preparation Time: 15 minutes

Serves: 2

Calories: 300 **Sugar:** 4g **Sodium:** 400mg

Ingredients:

200g Chicken breast

100g Greek yogurt

Bell pepper

100g Cherry tomatoes

50g Feta cheese

Method of Preparation:

1. Season chicken breast with salt and pepper, then grill or pan-fry until fully cooked.
2. Dice the cooked chicken into bite-sized pieces.

3. In a bowl, mix Greek yogurt and crumbled feta cheese. Add a pinch of salt for taste.

4. Cut the bell pepper in half and remove seeds.

5. Stuff each pepper half with the Greek yogurt and feta mixture.

6. Arrange the stuffed peppers on a plate and top them with diced chicken and cherry tomatoes.

Chicken Caesar Salad

Preparation Time: 20 minutes

Serves: 2

Calories: 350 **Sugar:** 2g **Sodium:** 600mg

Ingredients:

200g Chicken thighs

Romaine lettuce (1 head, chopped)

Caesar dressing (4 tbsp)

Parmesan cheese (50g, shaved)

Cherry tomatoes (100g, halved)

Method of Preparation:

1. Cook chicken thighs until fully done and shred them into bite-sized pieces.
2. In a large bowl, combine shredded chicken, chopped romaine lettuce, and cherry tomatoes.
3. Add Caesar dressing to the bowl and toss the ingredients until evenly coated.
4. Top the salad with shaved Parmesan cheese.

Turkey Meatballs with Zucchini Noodles

Preparation Time: 25 minutes

Serves: 3

Calories: 280 **Sugar:** 5g **Sodium:** 450mg

Ingredients:

Ground turkey (300g)

Zucchini (2, spiralized into noodles)

Almond flour (2 tbsp)

Tomato sauce (200g, no added sugar)

Italian seasoning (1 tbsp)

Method of Preparation:

1. Preheat the oven to 375°F (190°C).

2. In a bowl, mix ground turkey with almond flour and Italian seasoning.

3. Form the mixture into meatballs and place them on a baking sheet.

4. Bake the meatballs in the preheated oven for 15-20 minutes or until fully cooked.

5. In a pan, heat tomato sauce, add zucchini noodles, and cook until noodles are tender.

6. Serve the turkey meatballs on top of the zucchini noodles.

Chicken Meatballs with Coconut Herb Sauce

Preparation Time: 30 minutes

Serves: 4

Calories: 250 **Sodium:** 400mg

Ingredients:

Ground chicken

Coconut milk

Fresh herbs (such as cilantro or parsley)

Garlic powder

Salt and pepper

Method of Preparation:

1. Preheat your oven to 375°F (190°C).
2. In a mixing bowl, combine ground chicken, chopped fresh herbs, garlic powder, salt, and pepper. Mix until well combined.
3. Shape the mixture into small meatballs and place them on a baking sheet.
4. Bake the meatballs in the preheated oven for about 20-25 minutes or until fully cooked.
5. In a saucepan, heat coconut milk over low heat. Add more fresh herbs, salt, and pepper to taste.
6. Once the meatballs are cooked, place them in the coconut herb sauce, allowing them to simmer for a few minutes.

7. Serve the chicken meatballs with the coconut herb sauce, and enjoy!

Zoodle Stir Fry

Preparation Time: 20 minutes

Serves: 2

Calories: 180 **Sodium:** 500mg

Ingredients:

Zucchini noodles (zoodles)

Shrimp or chicken, cooked

Soy sauce (or tamari for a gluten-free option)

Sesame oil

Garlic, minced

Method of Preparation:

1. Heat sesame oil in a large skillet over medium heat.
2. Add minced garlic and sauté until fragrant.
3. Add cooked shrimp or chicken to the skillet and stir-fry for a couple of minutes.

4. Add zucchini noodles (zoodles) to the skillet and stir-fry until they are just tender but still have a slight crunch.

5. Pour soy sauce over the zoodle mixture and toss until everything is well coated and heated through.

6. Serve the zoodle stir fry immediately.

Kung Pao Chicken

Preparation Time: 25 minutes

Serves:3

Calories: 300 **Sodium:** 600mg

Ingredients:

Chicken breast, diced

Peanuts, unsalted

Bell peppers, diced

Soy sauce

Sriracha sauce

Method of Preparation:

1. In a wok or large skillet, cook diced chicken until browned and cooked through.
2. Add diced bell peppers to the wok and stir-fry until they are slightly tender.
3. Toss in unsalted peanuts, soy sauce, and sriracha sauce. Stir until the sauce evenly coats the chicken and peppers.
4. Continue to cook for a few more minutes until everything is well combined and heated through.
5. Serve the Kung Pao Chicken over cauliflower rice or on its own.

Keto Pasta with Lemon Kale Chicken

Preparation Time: 20 minutes

Serves: 2

Calories: 400 **Sugar:** 5g **Sodium:** 150mg

Ingredients:

8 oz (227g) spiralized zucchini or other keto-friendly pasta substitute

2 boneless, skinless chicken breasts

1 bunch of fresh kale, stems removed and leaves chopped

1 lemon, juiced

2 tablespoons olive oil

Method of Preparation:

1. Season the chicken breasts with salt and pepper.
2. In a skillet, heat 1 tablespoon of olive oil over medium heat. Add the chicken breasts and cook until browned and cooked through (about 5-7 minutes per side).
3. Remove the chicken from the skillet, and in the same skillet, add another tablespoon of olive oil.
4. Add the chopped kale to the skillet and sauté until wilted.
5. Slice the cooked chicken breasts into strips and add them back to the skillet along with the spiralized zucchini.
6. Drizzle the lemon juice over the mixture, toss everything together, and cook for an additional 2-3 minutes.
7. Serve immediately.

Mini Eggplant Pizza

Preparation Time: 30 minutes

Serves: 4

Calories: 180 **Sugar:** 3g **Sodium:** 250mg

Ingredients:

2 small eggplants, sliced into rounds

1 cup sugar-free tomato sauce

1 cup shredded mozzarella cheese

1/4 cup grated Parmesan cheese

1 tablespoon olive oil

Method of Preparation:

1. Preheat the oven to 400°F (200°C).
2. Place the eggplant rounds on a baking sheet and brush both sides with olive oil.
3. Bake the eggplant rounds for 10-12 minutes, flipping halfway through, until they are tender.
4. Remove the eggplant from the oven and spread a spoonful of tomato sauce on each round.

5. Sprinkle mozzarella and Parmesan cheese on top of the tomato sauce.

6. Return to the oven and bake for an additional 8-10 minutes, or until the cheese is melted and bubbly.

7. Remove from the oven and let it cool for a few minutes before serving.

Broccoli, Asparagus, and Celery Salad

Preparation Time: 15 minutes

Serves: 4

Calories: 120 **Sugar:** 3g **Sodium:** 60mg

Ingredients:

2 cups broccoli florets

1 cup asparagus spears, chopped

2 celery stalks, thinly sliced

1/4 cup olive oil

2 tablespoons apple cider vinegar

Method of Preparation:

1. Steam or blanch the broccoli and asparagus until they are crisp-tender.
2. In a large bowl, combine the broccoli, asparagus, and sliced celery.
3. In a small bowl, whisk together the olive oil and apple cider vinegar to create the dressing.
4. Pour the dressing over the vegetables and toss to coat.
5. Serve chilled.

Spicy Lemon Ginger Chicken Soup

Preparation Time: 20 minutes

Serves: 4

Calories: 150 **Sugar:** 1g **Sodium:** 300mg

Ingredients:

2 boneless, skinless chicken breasts, shredded

4 cups chicken broth (preferably low sodium)

1 tablespoon grated fresh ginger

1 lemon, juiced

1 teaspoon red pepper flakes (adjust to taste)

Method of Preparation:

1. In a pot, bring the chicken broth to a simmer.
2. Add the shredded chicken, grated ginger, and red pepper flakes to the simmering broth.
3. Cook for 10-15 minutes, allowing the flavors to meld.
4. Just before serving, squeeze the lemon juice into the soup and stir.
5. Taste and adjust the seasoning as needed.
6. Serve hot.

CONCLUSION

In conclusion, Low carb diets have been associated with several health benefits such as; weight loss and blood sugar levels management.

The recipes provided are designed to be simple, delicious, and low in carbohydrates.

With just a handful of wholesome ingredients, each recipe encapsulates the essence of mindful eating without compromising on flavor.

Now that you've come to the end, I hope these easy-to-follow recipes have not only tantalized your taste buds but have also helped you to embrace a low-carb lifestyle effortlessly.

Whether you are a seasoned chef or a kitchen novice, this book is designed to make your culinary adventures not only accessible but also delightful.

Made in the USA
Las Vegas, NV
26 September 2024

95807790R00036